teach me about

Listening

Copyright © Joy Berry, 2022
Originally Published, 1986

All rights are reserved.

No part of this book can be duplicated or used without the prior written permission of the copyright owner, except for the use of brief quotations from the book.

For inquiries or permission requests contact the publisher.

Published by Joy Berry Enterprises
www.joyberryenterprises.com

teach me about

By JOY BERRY

Illustrated by Bartholomew

I cannot see sounds but I listen and hear sounds coming from

- inside me,
- above me,
- below me,
- in front of me,
- in back of me, and
- to the side of me.

Some sounds are close to me.

Others are far away.

Almost everything I do

makes a sound.

Sometimes I listen and

I hear sounds that are made

by **people.**

Sometimes I listen and

I hear sounds that are made

by **animals.**

Sometimes I listen and

I hear sounds that are made

by **nature.**

Sometimes I listen and

I hear sounds that are made

by **machines.**

Sometimes I listen and

I hear sounds that are made

by **tools.**

Sometimes I listen and

I hear sounds that are made

by **toys.**

Sometimes I listen and

I hear sounds that are made

by **musical instruments.**

Some musical instruments

play a **melody** sound.

Some musical instruments play a **rhythmic** sound.

Some of the sounds I hear are **soft.**

Other sounds are **loud.**

Some of the sounds I hear

are **high.**

Other sounds are **low.**

Sometimes I listen and I hear an **echo.**

I make a sound.

I hear it.

Then, I hear it again.

Some of the sounds I hear

are **pleasant.**

These sounds make me feel good.

Some of the sounds I hear

are **unpleasant.**

These sounds bother me.

Sometimes everything around me is quiet.

There are no sounds.

I listen and there is **silence.**

helpful hints for parents about
Listening

Dear Parents:

The purpose of this book is
- to define the function of the ears in regard to a child's auditory perception of the world, and
- to help children develop the sensory awareness that is fundamental to all learning.

You can best implement the purpose of this book by
- reading it to your child, and
- reading the following *Helpful Hints* and using them whenever applicable.

SOUNDS

Newborns
Mother's heartbeat is the most familiar sound to a newborn. A soft rhythmic sound which simulates the maternal heartbeat can have a calming effect on an irritable baby. Loud or sudden noises will startle a young baby. Surround your newborn with soothing sounds like soft music, but don't alter the natural sounds of your family's routine since your baby will need to adjust to them.

Quality not quantity
Infants show a preference for sounds in the normal human voice range. Babies exhibit rhythmic body movements in response to their mothers' speech patterns. Researchers believe this rhythmic patterning may be the rudiment of human speech development. Talking and singing to your baby form important communication bonds through sound. Besides talking to your baby, you may want to provide sound stimulation by using the following:

- Recorded sounds and music. Special recordings of sounds in the womb are available to soothe newborns. Play a variety of music and observe your baby's preferences.
- Music boxes and wind-up music players. These provide a repetition of sounds that appeals to infants.
- Wind chimes. These can create a soft, familiar sound for your baby's environment.
- Bells, rattles, or sound makers. When securely attached to baby's crib, these provide a connection between sound and movement. Be sure they are out of reach.
- Singing to your baby.

Noise
Be discriminating about the sounds in your baby's environment. Stimulate hearing, but avoid overwhelming your baby with noise. If too many sound sources are present at once, the infant can't distinguish the sounds and

they become a confusion of noise. Avoid exposing your baby to sound confusion when control of the environment is possible.

HEARING

Causes of hearing loss
A number of factors are responsible for hearing loss in children:

Prenatal factors
Prenatal factors such as
- rubella in the mother during pregnancy,
- Rh blood type incompatibility, or
- premature birth

can cause hearing loss from birth.

Environmental factors
Environmental factors are also responsible for childhood hearing losses. These may include
- injury to the ear or skull
- high fever from diseases such as scarlet fever, mumps, whooping cough, or meningitis. Most of these childhood diseases are preventable through immunization.

Inherited factors
Some children are predisposed to hearing loss from inherited physiological factors.

Ear infections
- **Middle ear.** Most common ear problems are related to upper respiratory infections or allergies that affect the eustachian tubes of the ears. Blockage of the eustachian tubes can cause inflammation of the middle ear, and/or fluid in the middle ear.
  These conditions are indicated by irritation or pain in the ear and/or fever, usually following a cold. Crying, pulling the ear, and shaking the head may be indications of ear pain. If ear infection seems likely, seek medical

attention for your child. Middle-ear infections can be successfully treated with antibiotics and decongestants. Such treatment shortens the natural, often painful course of middle-ear disease and minimizes the risk of complications which can result in hearing impairment. Temporary hearing loss may result from ear infection but generally clears as the inflammation and fluid collection subsides. Check with your child's doctor if hearing impairment continues beyond the treatment period for ear infection.

- **Swimmer's ear.** Swimmer's ear is an infection of the external ear canal which can be quite common in the summer months. The condition is most likely a fungus infection contained within the skin of the ear canal up to the eardrum but is not usually present on the inside of the eardrum in the middle ear. Ear pain or itching that is sensitive to touch may indicate swimmer's ear. The condition should be evaluated by a physician who will likely prescribe eardrops as treatment.

Signs of hearing loss

Hearing loss can become apparent at any age. The following behavioral indicators may be symptoms of hearing loss:

Newborns
- If the baby is *not* startled by a loud noise such as a hand clap three to six feet away.
- If the baby, when crying, does *not* respond to soothing by the parent's voice.

At one year old
- If the child does *not* turn toward familiar sounds.
- If the child does *not* make sounds in response to verbal interaction with others.

At one-and-a-half years old
- If the child is *not* verbalizing a few simple words such as mama and daddy.
- If the child, when questioned, cannot identify by pointing to parts of the body.

At two years old
- If the child cannot follow simple verbal commands without visual prompting.
- If the child cannot repeat short phrases.

At three years old
- If the child cannot identify or locate the source of a sound.
- If the child cannot understand and use simple words like *me*, *big*, and *go*.

At four years old
- If the child cannot give a verbal account of a recent experience.
- If the child cannot carry out two consecutive verbal directions.

At five years old
- If the child cannot engage in simple conversation.
- If the child's speech is very hard to understand.

PROFESSIONAL EVALUATION

Any one of the above indications warrants a professional medical evaluation of your child's hearing ability. If there is a hearing problem it should be treated as soon as possible.

The family doctor

The first step in seeking professional evaluation of a hearing loss is to ask for a complete physical examination from your child's doctor. Be sure to express to the doctor your concerns about your child's hearing ability.

Specialists

Your doctor may refer you to a specialist for further examination.
Your child may be evaluated by
- a medical doctor who specializes in diagnosing and treating problems of the ear, nose, and throat (otorhinolaryngologist);
- a medical doctor who specializes in diagnosing and treating ear diseases (otologist); or
- a trained specialist who evaluates hearing problems (audiologist). Other specialists you may wish to consult for an evaluation of the effects of a hearing loss on your child include:

specially trained educators to determine learning problems;
a psychologist to evaluate any emotional problems;
a pediatrician to examine your child for possible related problems.

Community resources
Hearing evaluations are available in many communities at speech and hearing clinics connected with hospitals, universities, public schools, and national associations.

Early identification of hearing impairment is essential to proper speech development. Hearing ability is a prerequisite of listening ability.

LISTENING SKILLS
Your child's listening skill development is related to learning, speech, and reading skill development. Learning, speech, and reading play vital roles in your child's ability to communicate. From birth to age two is a crucial period in speech development. You can enhance your child's communication skills through training in listening skills.

Listening activities
Listening is a trainable activity which engages the attention and active intellectual participation of the listener. A variety of activities promote listening discrimination. The following activities can be done with children of approximately two to five years of age:

- **Reading.** Read to your child on a regular basis. Use a variety of reading sources. Supplement the reading with discussion and interaction with your child.
- **Sound containers.** Collect pairs of containers of various sizes from tennis ball or potato chip canisters to small 35 millimeter film containers or baby food jars. Fill the containers with items such as rice, salt, pebbles, sand, bells, beans, coins, and paper clips. Two cans filled with the same material will produce identical sounds. Cover the containers with lids and tape them shut. Mix up the containers and have your child match the pairs by shaking them and listening for the pairs that sound alike.
- **Echo chambers.** Encourage your child to experience an echo by vocalizing

into a large trash can, a large bucket, a shower stall, or an empty oatmeal box.

- **Familiar sounds.** Create familiar sounds for your child to identify. Have the child turned away or blindfolded while you create a variety of sounds such as snapping your fingers, whistling, turning on the faucet, tapping a glass with a spoon, opening and closing the refrigerator, crushing paper, turning on the vacuum cleaner, or flushing the toilet. Ask the child to identify each sound.
- **Animal sounds.** Imitate animal sounds or play a recording of animal sounds for your child to identify.
- **Loud and soft.** Introduce the concepts of loud and soft by experimenting with the volume control on a television, radio, or record player. Use the child's nose as an imaginary volume control on vocal sounds produced in loud and soft tones by the child.
- **Sound location.** Hide a ticking clock or a kitchen timer and ask your child to locate it by the sound. Increase the degree of difficulty as your child's listening discrimination improves.
- **Listening and movement.** Play a selection of music of varied rhythms, and encourage your child to move the way the music feels. Observe the changes in body movement as the musical rhythms change.
- **Music makers.** Create rhythm makers with a variety of materials including
  rolled sheets of paper   metal strainer and wooden spoon
  paper towel rolls   metal grater and wooden spoon
  sand paper   washboard and thimble
  pans and spoons   two spoons
  lid cymbals   brush and screen
  empty oatmeal box   paper cups
- **Outdoors.** Encourage sound discrimination outdoors by calling your child's attention to various sounds. Have your child identify sounds without looking. Distinguish such sound variations as loud and soft, high and low, and the source of sounds, such as human, animal, and machinery.

www.ingramcontent.com/pod-product-compliance
Lightning Source LLC
Chambersburg PA
CBHW081409070526
44583CB00020B/2745